Beautiful Broken Bits of Glass

Deora Inniss

BookLeaf
Publishing

India | USA | UK

Presentation by *BookLeaf Publishing*

Web: www.bookleafpub.com

E-mail: info@bookleafpub.com

ISBN: 978-93-5744-337-1

First edition 2022

DEDICATION

To Those Who Cry Alone and Those Too Numb
To Cry

ACKNOWLEDGEMENT

Many people did not have a safe haven to call their home as they grew up. I was lucky enough to have a mother and father who have encouraged me and fostered growth in every aspect of my life consistently and constantly. When I started to show signs that I struggled with mental illness they got me the help I needed immediately. I thank them for their unconditional love. I thank my little sister for reminding me that I am never too old for my imagination. I thank my little brother who is always there to lend a supportive hand. I thank my grandparents for encouraging my intelligence. I thank my best friend who helped me take the first step to get my collection of poetry to a publisher. Thank you to all of my friends who have listened to my poems, short stories, and novel ideas over the years with large smiles, listening ears, and open hearts. Finally, thank you Book Leaf Publishing for giving me the start I had only ever dreamed would happen.

PREFACE

This is literary piece is fictional and seems realistic and relatable because it is meant to be. It is supposed to invoke emotions such as pain, and sadness. It is also meant to invoke perseverance, dedication, and motivation. To all my readers, please keep going you have a story and someone wants to hear it.

Barbaric Body Dysmorphia

A beautiful, expensive, glass mirror hangs on
my bedroom door,
Pulling in, entrancing, deep from within my core
Intricate designs and engravings around the
metal frame,
Forgetting it's beauty as I see my hair is messy
and untamed,

Step closer gazing into the crystal,
Every second I feel my self-confidence become
distal,
Faded scars and bumps that lie beneath the hot
inflamed pimples,
No reason to smile, my acne ruins my dimples.

Slowly scanning my body in my reflection,
Attention inadvertently focused on every
imperfection,
My chest is too big, my hips have subtle dips
and I still have "baby fat"
Disgusting, appalling like those around me need
to be protected in full hazmat

Pushing out my stomach, I look childbearing,
Upset my thighs have gotten so big the rips in
my jeans keep tearing,
Built like a rectangular in fashion, a straight line
from my shoulders down,
People call me beautiful and I cannot help but to
frown.

Like a refrigerator broad and wide,
Perhaps, a wisdom tooth, roughly the same
length on every side.
Legs, built like tree trunks robust and bulking,
Shoulders, like a football player in full pads,
absolutely hulking.

Gaining weight too quickly much to my dismay,
Wishing I could go under the knife and have a
surgeon begin to cut away,
Some from my underarms, a lot from my
stomach and thighs,
Imaginably, then my self-esteem would finally
begin to rise.

Working out for hours a day until I feel sick,
That's how I know it is okay to stop, that's my
trick.

Nothing processed, no sugar, additives, animal
products or meat,
A strict diet and caloric count, I don't cheat.

My flat unrounded and unshapely hips,
Dismally, puberty did not me rid of the dips.
Overall, I am too flat to be considered
curvaceous,
Nevertheless, to call me "skinny" would be
audacious

Packing on the pounds day after day,
My face similar to a bacterial war zone I can't
keep at bay.
Tears slowly, steadily, silently streaming down
my face,
Reaching out towards the mirror and towards my
reflection to trace.

Lashing out in dejection and my fist hits the
glass,
Knees, feel weak, I sob and collapse
Cracks, breaches, fractures, and breaks
spiderweb through the image.
However, my mirror matches me accurately now
simply, damaged.

Impending Invasive Imaginations

The room is dark with no light in sight,
Daily, I become poisoned with more spite
Curled up defenselessly in the corner,
Everywhere, but my bedroom I feel like a
foreigner

Mascara running down my cheeks like a
depressing black river,
Promises, goals, dreams, and aspirations, I can't
deliver.
Spark of light, desire, ambition, and life was
engulfed in the dark long ago,
My brain is my preeminent foe.

I used to smile and make everyone laugh,
Now look into memories it is strangers in my
photographs
Now, I am anxious and unsettled by people
because of the hurt,
Sometimes getting out of bed and showering is
all the strength I can exert

A history of disappointment, anger, and abuse
has exhausted me.
From this mental prison, I want to be an escape
and free
Toxic, noxious people yell, scream, hit, and
harm
Thoughts of self-infliction, pain, and sabotage
begin to swarm

Nightly, crying myself to sleep.
Fearful, for the day I become too numb to weep
Like a depressing song stuck on repeat.
Pressures of life suffocate like a flame producing
white heat.

A burden, hopeless, and with no reason to live.
"No! Stop!" I tell myself as I try to find more to
give.
Unable to see a chance of having my dream job
or going to university.
I push the thought out of my head as I convince
myself to battle adversity

Perhaps the answer is in the bathroom as a bottle
of pills,
The mere suggestion gives me chills,
Screaming into my pillow sobbing, "Enough!"
"I'm tired of people telling me I'm tough"

Help! Someone, please! I'm so alone.
I can't do this, not on my own.
Unsure of what I need hospitalization, a
vacation, or medication.
Please, hear my cries and painful realization.

Decimation, Desolation and Devastation

My friends told me I need to relax,
An out, a way to distract myself from panic
attacks,
Late one Friday night after a football game,
That night changed the trajectory of my life I'm
no longer the same,

Walked up with three friends to the front door,
Later that night I would be traumatized, alone
and sore,
Music was blaring and vibrating with bright
colorful lights,
I tried to stay with my friends but they quickly
left my sight.

I was alone and you struck up a conversation,
You were cocky and arrogant about your skills
of flirtation,
You asked me if I was enjoying myself and I
lied,
You were the host and my lie only seemed to
boost your pride.

You suggested I check out your bedroom,
It didn't take a genius to what your goal was so I assumed.
I thank you and politely said no,
But you grabbed my arm refusing to let go,

I told you to let go and that your grip hurt.
You hastily let out an apology with a blurt,
Your friends came over to talk to you,
I didn't know their energy would help the chaos ensue

One offered me a cup with more Jack than with coke,
Another offered to take me outside and a joint we could smoke
I politely said, "No, I don't want a drink."
You pushed a second one towards me before I could think.

Everyone began to stare at me and encouraging to down it,
It smelled disgusting but I submitted against my better judgment,
You all surround me talking to me more with each refill,

The constant pressure to drink as my panic
started to spill,

You helped me find the bathroom as I began to
get sick,
I need to find my friends and get out of here
quick.
I opened up the door and you were there hunting
My brain foggy dazed and confused as I tried to
be confronting

No, I don't owe you anything.
Stop trying to convince me to do something.
He grabs me again. "No! I am not going upstairs
with you."
I yank myself away and I am tired of being
subdued.

In my state of intoxication and sedation
I realize his bedroom bathroom is my current
location.
You make snide remarks about me and the way I
look.
I hit you in the face as hard as I can but I know
its a weak left hook.

No! My dress isn't asking for trouble.

Get the hell away from me and my personal
bubble.
I wiggly and squirm but I am uncoordinated and
the ground is shifting,
I feel tired and my strength and focus are
drifting.

No means no! Get the fuck away from me!
Leave before I press charges of assault to the
first degree!
You ignore every plea, threat, cry, and rejection,
I feel as though I am defenseless against you, a
sickening infection.

You partially undress me when there's a knock at
the door,
I can barely move I am incredibly sore.
This is my chance to run to get away from this
beast,
With every second I wait my chances decrease

The light shines through onto the bed and his
attention switches,
I kick him and bite him as I grab my dress which
is nearly stitches.
I run out of the room, and fall down the stairs,
I don't stop running, not even when I feel the
cool night air

My bare feet pound the pavement as I stagger
ahead,
I grip my dress as it hangs by thread,
I begin to shiver and shake while I continue my
escape to authority,
I hope and I pray it will help this feeling of
inferiority.

Serial Self Inflicted Violence

Abstract art with a beautiful red ink,
A delicate canvas that brings me to the brink,
Carefully and precisely following each stroke,
Emphatically expressing my emotions as I try
not to choke

A masterpiece meant for me as an audience and
illustrator,
My inspiration describing me as a proliferator
Continually multiplying big and small
Trying to defend me behind broken walls

Things piling up and cascading down,
Emotions rarely shift from a frown,
Turning to my art as the pressure amounts,
Feeling as though nothing including myself
counts.

Slowly dragging metal to skin
Conceding to the need and letting temptation
win,
Locked away in my room
Solemnly seeking a nightmarish tomb

Desiring the pain and hurt to cease,
I would do anything to find inner peace
My secret is hidden by long pants and
long-sleeved shirts
One thing that relieves the hurt

When people talk about others with marks,
They make snide comments about worshipping
demons in the dark
I feel as though I'm succumbing to the negatives
and dread
The darkest place I know clearly is my head

Twilight Trepidation Trance

Stuck, lodged, jammed, deep in your throat.
Suffocating like someone in the ocean hoping
for a lifeboat,
Heart racing, with fear, terror, and panic,
Feeling lost and broken looking for a personal
mechanic,

Entering your lungs, you can't breathe.
Helpless, hopeless, useless as you seethe,
Drowning, suffocating, choking,
Angst, terror, rage, despair and provoking,

I can't move, stuck, paralyzed,
So many emotions, your insides brutalized,
Unable to kick, scream, bite, or claw
"I can't do this," its the final straw

I can't flee, a deer in the headlights.
At the final moment fleeing into the night
A flash from your past as the lights go by,
The memories and mental scars internally
crucify

A memory you would rather forget
Transitioning your mindset to a plot and an
epithet
The things you face in only your nightmares
Hoping, praying, begging, for someone to give
you care.

Deeply Drowning Into Disaster

Vibrant red, mundane brown, and shimmering
gold leaves line the trees,
The air, cool and crisp yet I find it hard to
breathe,
I've become familiar with flora at this place,
A secluded hideaway to replace my current
headspace,

A vibrant, green grass soft to the touch
A safe haven where for once life doesn't feel
like too much,
However, all beautiful things, abruptly end,
The water of a pond halts the meadow so it
cannot overextend

The water is dark and murky unreflective and
hidden in shadow,
One foot, two feet, I step in believing it is
shallow,
Whoosh! Frigid temperatures encompass my
body as the bottom disappears,
The surface is no longer near,

Violently flapping my arms like a bird does their
wings,
Shaking and screaming as I feel the darkness
creep and cling,
Unable to move forward, is it possible to go
deeper
Is this the place I will meet the Grimm Reaper?

Silence, the calm before the storm, tranquility,
Struggle to move, exhaustion has taken my
ability
Mind drifting to the idea of an eternal nap,
Memories of my past begin to quickly overlap,

A sudden surge of energy allows me to break the
surface,
Clawing my way to land as I emerge with
purpose,
Coughing up water and sludge as I clear my
lungs,
Terrifying realistic concept that my life can end
so shortly after it's begun

Inhaling on the shore as my chest rises and as it
falls,
Screaming out for help, for hope, for someone,
but no one hears my calls,

If a girl screams alone in the woods does it make
a sound?
In my mind and on land I nearly drowned.

Plop! The lighter goes into the abyss,
Next, I throw in the flower with great dismiss,
The escape now the penitentiary,
How much longer can I survive this 21st
century?

Breaking to the Bitter End

Waiting for the sound of the parents to come to a
halt,
Blaming myself because I use self-judgment by
default,
Suffering psychologically,
A plan against my religious ideology.

Spiraling further than I believed feasible,
Feeling as though my existence is no longer
appealable,
No longer possessing a will to inhale,
Internal agony never-ending wales,

Leaving an envelope stuffed with a thick long
letter,
Taking a deep breath as I remind myself this is
for the better,
Tidying up my room with a few final tweaks,
Deep breaths and deep thoughts about my final
week,

A bottle of pills on the shelf,
This is it, I am ready to kill myself,

My one regret is my parents will find me and be
in distress
Soon from this plane, I will quickly transgress

I finish the bottle with a large Gulp! of water,
I apologize quietly for being a bad daughter,
This is the capacity.
To continue, I don't have the audacity,

So, this time I create art with all of my pain,
Pretty effortless with no need to strain
Up and down with a shard from the mirror, in
deep long strokes
I cry out in pain and choke,

I know the end is near and I don't regret it,
For I know I will be at peace and my art and
cocktail is to credit.
I grab my favorite stuffed animal and a photo,
This is it, this is the way I want to go.

My stuffed rabbit reminds me how things used
to be fun,
Now as I begin to cry it is settling in what I have
done,
I look at the photo of my family I took on my
Polaroid,

I begin to cry harder as I realize my world is
finally destroyed

Curling up into a fetal ball,
Waiting for sleep as I look at the wall,
Slowly but surely my eyes begin to get heavy,
Thank God, there is no more pain I have to levy.

One Step Forward

Making the most of what I can,
Constantly and consistently tired of being less
than
Waking up in the morning find one reason to
smile
Harder, when I feel as though I'm reminded the
world is vile

Not knowing to eat, would be harder than to
retch
Relieving the anguish slowly through sketch
after sketch,
No longer using drugs,
Even though temptation tugs.

Tough skin, beginning to scar, not as lacerated,
Secluded from the negative influence safely
isolated,
Sleeping more but waking throughout the night,
A glass of water, several deep breaths,
convincing myself I'm alright.

Ask for help it will be given,
Centralizing my focus trying to remain driven
At night the window stays closed
Some of the few ways I try to keep my mind
composed

Resentment Towards Remedial Treatment

Sitting in a little waiting room with walls of
beige and white,
Refusing to want to be here feeling angry and
needing something to smite,
Into an intake room and go through their process
Trying to stay positive and thinking of this as a
step towards progress

Embarrassed, ashamed, and full of regret,
Perceiving medical professionals all as
psychological threats,
Meeting the doctor, answering questions with
one word.
The doctor told me if I want to get better I can't
act so absurd.

Mandated to therapy to talk about my feelings,
Thoughts of people's judgment have my mind
reeling.
Worrying I will run into someone else I know
here,
After all, we all live in a very tiny sphere.

Reminding myself it is better than the hospital
substitute
Not shaking myself of the reason I feel destitute,
So many problems and I really worth the time,
Anxiety, Depression, PTSD, and being the
victim of a crime

I see a specialist to help with the conceptions of
my body,
Rolling my eyes, while practicing exercises
about how I look, how to be somebody
I see another person to help me regulate my
mood,
Surprisingly, my depression is one of the central
points for being rude

Anxious from life feeling suffocating and
crushing,
Overwhelmed, I struggle to maintain hygiene
like hair brushing
Not entirely alone because all these
professionals have multiple clients,
Instead of feeling like a bug, they slowly
empower me making me feel giant

Agonizing Anniversary

I am not lying! Please hear my cries!
The only things that come out of his mouth are
lies!
"Look, I know he and I are different in every
way.
But that does mean he should get away with the
deed he did that day!"

He is rich, a varsity jock, and white.
"Judge, what did you mean by I should have put
up more of a fight?"
I don't remember what happened because I was
drugged.
Too many beers, too fast, I chugged.

Blacked out, unconscious, and vulnerable.
That is when he realized I was available!
I know, I'm black but please no stereotypes
please be kind.
Grr, how I wish I could give you a piece of my
mind.

"A slap on the wrist? That's what he gets? An acquittal?" I quit.
I hate how in this society my basic human decency. I must submit.

Beautiful Bits of Broken Glass

The feminine desire to look beautiful in my
mirror,
The goal is to one day look into it clearer.
Carefully removing it from my door and put it in
the trash,
Accidentally gashing on beautiful bits of broken
glass and the urge spreads through me like a rash

Running to the bathroom and washing the blood
in the sink,
Ending it all or leaving small unobservable
marks are of all I can think,
Pouring, some disinfectant alcohol on it and it
burns a little bit
It feels painful, I like it, I hate to admit it.

Guilty, I can't hide the cut it is in the crease of
my hand,
Unnecessary guilt, because it was unplanned.
Then again, I didn't plan on existing on this
plane any longer.
As I cover the wound I wonder, if I or the urge is
stronger.

Repulsive Reflective Rollercoaster

Replacing the mirror with a new one but it didn't
stay,
Ideals of my body were too negative it had to go
away.
I covered it up with paper and tape,
All of them, little notes to myself on a
background of beautiful landscape

Telling myself I may not be beautiful in the
mirror but maybe inside,
A shallow lie and my tears begin to well up in
my eyes,
Knowing I talk too much, blunt, fast, and
abrasive,
People call me manipulative, my parents call it
persuasive.

Honest with intent and with my actions,
Nevertheless, genuinely bad at retractions.
If I was taken I know I would be scared,
But would anyone notice, listen to my warning
or would they care?

Am I narcissistic? As I look at my body as she
changes and shifts,
Further damaging my mentality or is it sewing
rifts?
Removing so many people like cleaning my
closet in the spring,
Bringing in new friends so it is like I am
updating everything.

Interests have changed, I work and pay attention
in class,
Sometimes out the corner of my eye, I see a
reflection in the window glass,
Realizations that I hate the person I became.
It took so long for me to change

Who I am hates who I have been,
Soon who I am will only be a fill-in,
I will be the hero of my own story,
That is, at least, if first life doesn't destroy me

Cathartic Canvas Creations

In the past creating with paper, sharpies, colored
pencils and pens,
Loving the bright colors of the rainbow and
would use them time and time again.
Making my work bright, like my heart.
Seeing the world through childlike naivete as
beautiful art

Art style slowly shifted because my heart
absorbed darkness
Looking at the beginning of my sketchbook to
the end I see the starkness
Devolving to more creative unconventional
tools,
Becoming my own personal canvas but hiding
artwork at home and at school.

The thought of sharp razors, blood, and my skin.
For a while, I never thought I was going to win.
I tried different tricks and tips to get me to stop.
To combat the ideas I transformed my bedroom
into an art workshop.

Paint smoothly, and effortlessly glided through
my creations,
Cathartic seeing things come together even
when I felt devastation,
Learning new skills with charcoal and chalk,
Creating everything from the bottom of the
ocean to a moonwalk

Pain and hurt slowly drifting away,
As I paint an ice cream cone melting on a
summer day,
Glorious, swirls and sprinkles on top of sweet
cream,
Healthier outlet than letting out screams

Psychotropic Substances Session

I cannot keep going on this current treatment,
Counseling appointments are fine but rather
frequent,
Medication, I have started to take has been
slightly problematic,
Stating my opposition clearly without being
overdramatic.

Voicing my concerns clearly and attentively,
Every word and phrase presented tentatively
Carefully, walking the tightrope between
freedom and hospitalization,
Every word is a revelation and a hesitation.

Starting a new medication about a month back,
Now when my depression and anxiety hit it's
like a sneak attack,
From behind, feeling vile thoughts run rampant
and air stolen from my lungs,
Remembering my words are important and I
must be careful of my tongue

The doctor quickly types things out while
listening to my descriptions
Surprisingly, the doctor listens and changes the
prescription
Questiong, why she believed me so easily,
She can tell I am trying to live peacefully

No medication works the same for their client
population,
If it did, surely, it would undergo speculation
and investigation
Some times it takes one try other times ten,
The important thing is it should relieve, not
amplify time and time again

Secret Society of Self Care

Through the recent past, I struggled, finding,
energy to shower and get dressed,
Still, Some days I struggle, but what can I say
life is a mess.
Wanting to look, act and be modern-day royalty
In order to grow, I have to face my reality

Waking up in the morning as the light cascades
from outside,
Dragging myself out of bed not bushy-tailed nor
bright-eyed.
Plopping down to my floor, not in a ball, but
sitting upright,
Meditation, to help with the insufferable terrors
of the night

Next stop, the shower my secret song sanctuary,
I am very strong but a tune is not something I
can carry.
Stepping out, washing my face over the sink,
brush my teeth and hair,
I remember for a long time I didn't have the
energy and I didn't care.

My mental health is my priority now instead of
pleasing others.
Learning the hardest way and don't think I need
to learn another,
Scheduling time weekly for a self-service spa
night.
Sometimes its facemasks, hair masks, for peels
or nails that shine bright

Other times my self-care is going out and trying
something new,
Restaurants, hiking trails, road trips, because I
need a change of view.
Letters, I write to my future self to show my
growth,
To keep going, succeeding or failing, to try is
my personal oath

Tell Tale Triggers

No mirrors in my room anymore,
Knowing I have gotten better but you can never
be too sure,
Unistalling social media on my devices,
Mental health is priceless.

No longer comparing myself to girls out in the
community,
Brain, slowly, battling body dysmorphia with
immunity,
To shave, I no longer use razor blades,
Intentional behavior changes I use as a defensive
brigade.

Sticky notes cover my walls with positive
affirmations,
Negative comments and social media affect my
mental narrations,
Nervous, when I interact with people from my
past,
Anxiety still washes over me but I have coping
mechanisms so it doesn't last

Unable to say the name of my abuser to this day,
The silence I think states all I need to say,
Loved ones avoid words, phrases, situations.
Upholding my expectations while strengthening
my foundation.

Unable to watch horror movies due to graphic
sex assault scenes,
Changes in my diet, eating regularly and
reintroducing proteins
Avoid parties to enjoy games, crafts, cards, and
movies with friends,
I practice my self-care when I feel the need to
cleanse.

Solemnly Swimming

Working hard to get back into something I
enjoyed,
Once, something that I destroyed.
Opening the deep dark blue combination locker,
People greet me but today I am not much of a
talker,

A five year anniversary since I tried to end it all,
I have grown so much and I am able to stand
tall,
The scars are deep jagged and visible, especially
as I strip down,
My cover-up slowly slips down until it hits the
ground.

I never thought I would be comfortable so
exposed,
The first time I tried to put on a swimsuit I
couldn't stay composed.
The idea of fabric clinging to my skin barely
shielding me from the world,
It made me feel weak and vulnerable like when I
was a little girl,

Flip flops clip, clop, as I walk around the edge,
Feeling the urge to swiftly jump off the ledge,
Following it as I happily become submerged.
Feeling the serotonin levels in my body begin to
surge

Swimming down the lane and back, as my stress
glides away
Simply, swimming instead of deeply drowning
day after day
The crystal, clear chlorinated pool,
Knowing my limits and listening to my body is
the first rule

Some days I am here for minutes and other days
hours,
No matter what my mood I never leave here
sour.
The water works magic as it clears my mind and
soothes my soul,
Making me feel weightless and buoyant as the
world tried to take its toll.

Improvement In Interpersonal Intimacy

It's been years and I am still scared of men,
Every date I will find a flaw or a red flag again
and again,
Never giving them a true chance, running from
the principle
Remembering the formidable and working to
sustain my invincible,

A supportive friend from my youth to adulthood,
Comforting, waiting always making sure I am
understood,
He doesn't pry and I have told him about my
history,
He isn't judgemental only wants to protect me
from additional misery,

Alarm bells ringing in my head screaming away
from him and love to run,
If we keep score it's me zero, him one,
Never rushing or pushing simply waiting for me
to be ready
The idea makes me nervous but with him, I've
never felt unsteady

He makes me feel comfortable always asking for
permission,
He lets me have control never forcing me into
submission
Questions and clarifies, always asking for my
consent,
Humanity, boundaries, and decency I'm never
forced to relent

It seems as though the bar is on the floor for my
expectations,
Positive or negative he always respects my
declarations
Some days I am okay with more other days less
Sometimes I am okay only to be hand in hand
other days I can undress

It's been years I have been with him and he
never fails,
When my nightmares persist he wakes me up
and prevails,
In a moment of terror in a moment of intimacy,
He does nothing but responds as he should,
chivalrously

Thorugh the ups and the downs he has been by
my side,

No matter what even when I backslide,
A warm embrace tight but not confined,
A beautiful safe haven we together have crafted
and designed

No means no and yes means yes,
I've never been in danger or physical distress
I have my autonomy with school, work, and
money,
I'm not called a "slut" or a "whore" but now
"babe" and "honey",

I have never been hit, neglected, gaslit, or
manipulated,
It's nice to be supported and encouraged instead
of deflated,
There is no more screaming, yelling, or
derogatory words,
Although I won't admit it we are two love birds

I am safe in my home and I am secure in my
bed,
Crazy to think, now, was my dreams when I
wanted to be dead
The mental battle, no longer on the forefront of
my mind,
My life and his beautifully intertwined.

I have grown so much from where I began,
From feeling nervous and crying all over the
man,
Living, loving, and having peace of mind,
I am glad his love is refined yet unconfined.

Shiny, Sparkling Stain Glass

Time has passed, I have flourished,
Thanks to a positive mental state I have
nourished,
Making it through high school all the way to my
doctoral degree,
Working with people who feel like me,

Nurturing, teaching with kindness and care,
Guiding and giving techniques while they are
stuck in despair,
Occasionally my lab coat rolls up the sleeve,
Patients catch a glimpse of my scars and know I
understand what they perceive

Periodically I feel as though I am stained,
Then I am more focused on the positive outlook
I must maintain,
Sporadically, I feel torn and stitched and patched
Nevertheless, I focus on the things that in this
world I feel attached

Daily, driving past a church on my commute,
Beautiful, bold, intricate, electrifying colored
windows, art, without dispute

Shiny, Sparkling stain glass, each piece
individually held together by a seam,
Realization, of past beautiful bits of broken
glass, and broken self-esteem

I have metamorphosized into beautiful stain
glass that allows me to glitter, gleam and beam

Words of Wisdom From a Wandering Soul

Too many people feel alone and forgotten,
A chaotic, messy, world filled with insufferable
toxins
Battling mental illness is exhausting but pivotal
Mental health, of the utmost importance and
unequivocal
Work can be too many hours in a week,
School can be so draining after studying its
difficult to speak
You deserve help, peace, and coping
mechanisms,
Don't listen to stigmas or other criticisms,
A mental illness does not have to dictate your
life,
It won't be easy and you will face some strife.
You are never any less of a person because of
the battle in your head,
You are a person with dreams, goals, aspirations,
and a whole life ahead.
Not everyone has a home that is safe and sound,
Some people are abused and others have to sleep
on the ground
No matter what your story or confrontations,

You deserve to have people in your life with
positive relations
Your body is beautiful no matter what you think,
You're practically, pretty, and perfect, don't let
your self-esteem, shrink,
People fear talking to professionals because of
grippy sock vacations,
There is always someone who wants you or
needs you please have that realization.